AGILE SOLUTIONS FOR THE PROJECT MINDED

DISCLAIMER

ISBN: 978-1-7357952-0-1

Printed by:
Power Of Purpose Publishing
www.PopPublishing.com
Atlanta, Ga. 30326

CONTENTS

CHAPTER 1

PROJECT MANAGEMENT BASICS

In a fiercely competitive business environment, a significant chunk of the work is project-based. It is a prized skill to deploy projects while:

- ✓ Aligning it with business goals
- ✓ Delivering it within the budget.
- ✓ Completing it on time.

This is why the role of project managers is of the utmost significance – a complex task awaits them. Project management requires them to have an analytical mind, organizational skills, and interpersonal abilities.

DEFINING A PROJECT

Before going deeper into project management, let's go over the concept of 'project'. Simply put, a project refers to a temporary job that is performed to generate a unique result, service, or product. Temporary is an important keyword; it means that the project must have a **beginning and an end**. This also implies that you can't categorize it under ongoing operations.

A project must have three basic attributes:

- ✓ Timeline

✓ Scope
✓ Resources

Let's go back to the project's purpose that focuses on creating a "unique result, service, or a product". What this signifies is that a project is kicked off to achieve a specific goal. It is not part of the routine day-to-day business processes. Additionally, it can also include a workforce that wasn't working before and can gather resources that weren't previously used.

For example, let's say you are managing a team of software developers that primarily develop web applications – And for now, you might have been developing enterprise back-end systems in Java; but then a client asks you to include a recommendation system that is highly reliant on machine learning. After assessing client requirements for a while, you decide to go out of your comfort zone and select the most popular language for machine learning – Python. However, you don't have a senior Python developer, so the project requires you to include a new member.

Before undertaking a project, keep the following factors in mind:

- Goal – What do you aim to accomplish with the project? It must be realistic. A startup cannot set off to develop a search engine like Google right from the beginning.
- Budget – Determine the cost of your project.
- Stakeholders – Make a list of all the key players (clients, partners, vendors, etc.).

- Timeline – The time required to complete and deploy the project.
- Project Manager – Appoint an individual who is responsible and answerable for the project.

DEMYSTIFYING PROJECT MANAGEMENT

Based on your client requirements, the art of combining the right knowledge, techniques, tools, and skill sets to a project is known as project management. It is a lot challenging to find the right blend of resources. For instance, imagine a scenario where you are tasked to create a social media app.

- You have adequate knowledge of how to create a mobile app and can make important decisions, such as whether to design a native app or a hybrid app.
- You have installed the right tools and set up the hardware that can easily process the intensive computing that is prevalent with mobile development. You have also set up the suitable IDEs and configured them (e.g. Android Studio, Xcode, etc.).
- Your team members have the mastery of the latest programming techniques.
- However, not all team members have the right skill sets. One of the inexperienced developers fails to write efficient code. While the app works for the moment, but when it reaches more than 100,000 users, then scalability issues can emerge. An inspection at that point can detect issues with the code, pointing the inexperienced developer as a culprit.

Project management is primarily geared towards identifying a problem. You can then design a proper plan to resolve it and go on to execute it flawlessly, in a bid to find a working solution.

Project management is not a product of modern times. In its raw form, it can be traced to ancient times. The marvels of humankind, such as the Pyramids of Giza and the Great Wall of China, were only made possible due to the use of project management.

The modern form of project management was developed during the 19th century. Planes were not discovered until then, which meant that railways were all the rage. Railway companies bought raw materials in massive quantities and took several employees under their wing. They were assigned to perform job duties for the "project" of the transcontinental railroad.

Frederick Taylor, one of the leading engineers in the 20th century, utilized project management concepts. Taylor was researching methods that would help him to increase industrial efficiency. He was dissatisfied with the existing solution; he did not support extending the work hours of laborers. Instead, he attempted to introduce smarter and more efficient strategies that were similar to some modern-day methods of project management.

Taylor's associate, Henry Gantt, advanced his work. He incorporated charts and bars to create graphs for different tasks involved in project management. In this way, Gantt was instrumental in visualizing the earlier form of project management.

As the Second World War broke out, industrial leaders and military around the world were committed to expanding production and innovation. Due to this, in-depth project management strategies came into place, which set the path for standardized processes.

After the end of the war, countries were focused on rebuilding their industries, these methods and processes surged in popularity throughout various industrial sectors. Afterward, the International Project Management Association and Project Management Institute were formed in 1965 and 1969, respectively.

At the turn of the 21st century, Agile Manifesto was created to codify the Agile project management methodologies.

STAGES OF PROJECT MANAGEMENT

The project management is divided into four stages. These are initiation, planning, execution, and closure. Sometimes, another phase is created from the third phase – Monitoring. Regardless of the exact number of stages, the underlying structure of project management works the same. Here is what each stage entails.

1. Initiation

To begin with; pick a business problem, need, or opportunity. Brainstorm for solutions that can solve an issue, meet a need, or seize an opportunity. Determine a project objective, evaluate whether the project is feasible enough, and find out the major project deliverables. Steps taken in the project initiation stage include the following:

- Undertake a feasibility study for identifying a problem.
- Identify the scope of the project.
- Identify deliverables and specify the service or product that you will offer.
- Identify project stakeholders and determine those who are affected by the project and list down their requirements.
- Focus on the development of a business case. Utilize the above criteria and compare the potential benefits and costs of the project.
- Create a statement of work. Write about the scope, objectives, and deliverables of the project.

2. Planning

After the project gets the green light based on its project initiation document, you can go ahead with the planning stage.

In this stage, you must split up a large project into smaller tasks. Next, build a team and form a schedule to finish assignments. Document smaller goals for a larger project and see to it that every goal can be achieved for a specific timeframe. Steps taken in the project planning stage include the following:

- Produce a project plan that identifies the following: project phases, possible constraints, project timeline, and the tasks to be completed.

- Design workflow diagrams. Use swim-lanes to visualize your processes. This can help to inform and communicate the role of each team member.
- Determine the budget and produce a financial plan. Rely on cost estimates to figure out the project spending. It is crucial to calculate the max ROI.
- Collect and gather resources. Assemble a functional team that includes both the external and internal talent pools. Also, make it a priority to ensure that each member possesses the essential tools to finish their tasks.
- Look out for risks, especially the standard quality roadblocks. Study the project in detail to detect issues that can put your project in a crisis. A risk management plan will help with mitigating risks, so that you can maintain the quality and timeline of the project.
- Arrange a kickoff meeting. Have your team attend it and give a basic project outline.

3. Execution

Your project is approved. You have developed a plan and briefed your team. Now is the time to get in action. The execution stages convert your intangible output plans to a real output or a working solution. The project manager plays a crucial role in this stage. They organize team members, track performance, manage deadlines and timelines, and ensure that work is done as per the original plan. Steps taken in the project execution stage include the following:

- Organize workflows and create tasks. The granular project parts are assigned to the relevant members.
- Arrange briefings for each task with your members. Provide an explanation of how different tasks work, offer essential guidance for task completion, and if required, arrange process-oriented training for the relevant team members.
- Communicate with the upper management, team members, and clients. Keep on updating the project to stakeholders regularly.
- Monitor work quality. Make it a priority that team members can work on tasks while meeting their required quality and time goals.
- Keep the budget in check. Monitor how much spending goes into the project.

Proper documentation adds a great deal of convenience to project execution.

Closure

You must enter the closure stage as soon as your team completes the project work.

Steps taken in the closure stage include the following:

- Analyze the performance of the entire project. Find out whether goals of the projects – task completion and delivery – were met. Prepare a checklist to verify the resolution of the initial problem.
- Assess the performance of your team members. Look into how they met their goals and review their work quality and timelines.

- Document project closure. Confirm that all project aspects were carried out. Tie up the remaining loose ends and send reports to the major stakeholders.
- Once the implementation phase ends, conduct reviews. It covers the entire project analysis, noting the lessons taught during the projects, which can come in handy in the future.
- Go through the accounting for the unused and used budget. If there's any resource that wasn't utilized, allocate it for future needs.

WHY IS PROJECT MANAGEMENT IMPORTANT?

Some parochial mindsets question the need for project management. They consider it as an unimportant overhead. To them, project management offers no value and instead slows down projects.

The reality is you cannot run projects without effective project management. It is vastly underrated. Good project management is not only about delivering the project in accordance with scope, budget, and time. It unites the teams and clients expertly, introduces a vision that can lead to success, and brings all the stakeholders on the same page. Here's why it is an important process.

1. Strategic Alignment

When done right, project managers bring real value to the table. Clients work with goals where project management is key to advancing those ambitions. Quality project management aligns the strategic goals of a business with the goals of the project.

While identifying a business case and determining its ROI, the role of project management is extremely valuable.

2. Realistic Project Planning

Project management adds a semblance of reality. It sets the right and realistic expectations on the deliverables: what must be delivered, when it must be delivered, and how much must be delivered.

If project management is not adopted, then over-ambitious project delivery timelines and budget estimates are approved. After some time, it is found that the project will not only get delivered late, but it has also exceeded the budget. Consequently, the future of the project will be in jeopardy.

3. Quality Controls

Project management keeps project quality in check and ensures that it consistently hits the mark. There's a considerable amount of pressure on the delivery of the project on time. Without project management, tighter schedules and rushed processes become the norm. As a result of this, the project stumbles due to poor output quality.

Project management guarantees that the project delivers on time without compromising on quality; it is tested at every stage.

4. Risk Management

Project management controls and mitigates risks. Risk management is critical to the success of a project. Sometimes, there's ample temptation to ignore knowing risks as the projects work. However, effective project management stops these risks from becoming issues.

Project managers identify and assess all the potential project risks. Risks are then quantified, so a mitigation strategy can be produced to counter them. Risks are prioritized based on their likelihood and severity and relevant responses are assigned to them.

CHAPTER 2

INTRODUCTION TO AGILE PROJECT MANAGEMENT

Whether you are curious about Agile project management or you have worked with it, you are well aware of the challenges faced by the project manager. It is hard to keep up with the modern, moody customer. They keep expecting quality software that must be completed on time within a pre-defined budget. What's more tricky and harder to manage is that sometimes requirements can change throughout the project lifecycle. Agile project management was introduced to address these concerns. It has gone on to become a leading project management methodology for a wide range of applications.

WHAT IS AGILE PROJECT MANAGEMENT?

Agile project management adopts an iterative approach for delivering a project throughout its lifecycle. Agile life cycles consist of multiple incremental steps or iterations that help you to complete a project. Iterative approaches are commonly implemented in software development to embrace adaptability and velocity.

One of the primary objects of an Agile approach is to provide value continuously throughout the process, rather than only providing benefits at the end. Agile project management is a value-driven methodology. It enables the delivery of high-quality and high-priority work to the stakeholders.

Agile project management is considerably different than the error-prone, costly, and plodding project management approaches of the past. Constant changes may overwhelm software projects. Customers are requested to approve requirements prior to the prototype testing. However, long delays and overhead expenses inflict damage to the project. Agile Project Management promotes change, regardless of how late it is introduced in the project. The onus is on the delivery of those features that is value-oriented, along with carrying critical information adequately. In this way, the scope, time, and cost of the project are managed terrifically.

A BRIEF HISTORY OF AGILE

In the 1990s, the software industry was reeling due to an unusual crisis. Many experts noted how the time taken from a validated business requirement to the working application in production extended to more than three years. Put simply, software projects were developed in more than three years!

The dilemma emerged because companies were growing at a rapid rate, but the state of existing software development was not good enough to meet their expanding requirements.

Three years is a long time where systems, requirements, and the business itself were prone to a plethora of changes. This led to the cancellation of different projects that failed after reaching a certain point. Although these projects were working fine in the beginning; but after a year or two, their requirements changed drastically – causing the project to shut down.

For some industries, software development required a greater time span. In the defense industry, a complex system could take 20 years to deploy. The Space Shuttle Program was created in 1982, but it employed the technology of the 1960s – more than two decades ago.

In the 1990s, John Kern, an aerospace engineer, had a hard time with this sluggish approach to software development. He was particularly frustrated at how the early decisions, taken in the project, couldn't be challenged later in the project lifecycle. His search for a responsive and timely framework inspired him to join a special group. The hugely talented group comprised 17 software experts who arrange informal meetings and discussed software development in detail. They were also trying to avoid going through the inefficient methods of waterfall methodology (one of the leading project methodologies) and other frameworks of the 20th century.

By 2001, a famous meeting was organized in Utah. Other than Kern, the participants included Alistair Cockburn, Arie van Bennekum, Ward Cunningham, Kent Beck, and a few more experts. Until that point, "Agile" was not brought up formally. The emphasis was placed on "lightweight" and "light" terms.

More specifically, these thought leaders looked for ways that could help them with rapid software development.

The idea was to provide the completed solution to the end-users quickly. There were two key benefits of this speedy approach. First, it ensured that users received business benefits quicker. Second, it helped the software team to receive quick feedback on the direction and scope of the software.

The willingness to change and rapid feedback leads to the formation of the major features of the Agile movement. For example, when the software team faces doubts regarding the user requirements, it produces a first approximation and studies the feedback. However, barely anything is set in stone at the start of the project.

Finally, these experts released and approved the Manifesto of Agile Software Development, marking the official creation of Agile.

CORE VALUES OF AGILE

You can follow Agile project management by understanding its four core values. These values are interlinked; they depend on each other to produce effective results. For instance, a team cannot implement a revision properly if they didn't prioritize communication. These values enable teams to work quickly and create optimized workflows. Here's a brief overview of the core Agile values.

1. Individuals and Interactions over Processes and Tools

This value prioritizes communication and teamwork. Traditionally, organizations create complex processes to complete projects. Although they are used to increase transparency between the workflows, they unintentionally create more delays and slow down the project progress. Similarly, the multi-layer hierarchy in organizations produces additional complications in the chain of demand and the project counters further delays.

On the other hand, Agile project management supports and promotes peer-to-peer communication. It empowers your team members to give precedence to effective communication, rather than depending excessively on tools and procedures throughout the project lifecycle.

Although these tools are useful, it is important to maintain productive interaction between stakeholders. It's the people who adapt to business requirements and drive the development process. If development is centered on tools, then it can make the team unresponsive to changes.

2. Working Software over In-Depth Documentation

This refers to the emphasis on creating working software over dedicating too much time to detailed documentation. This is another value that is focused on removing unmerited and unneeded delays.

In many projects, a significant chunk of the time goes into writing design documents, test plans, and technical specifications. The project manager is tasked to get the approval for these documents before work can begin on a working solution. Hence, this comprehensive documentation compels the team to spend their precious time on areas that are often irrelevant to the process.

Agile project management eliminates this barrier by streamlining documentation. It is structured such that the team receives a sufficient overview of the project. Therefore, they can start working on the project. While some of your members are developing a project's usable function, the remaining ones can brainstorm on how to optimize a process. Hence, productivity is increased to a significant extent.

Lastly, think from the perspective of the end-user. A customer is also going to like the sight of a working solution over a comprehensive document.

3. Customer Collaboration over Contract Negotiation

The Agile project management prevents the team from over-working on comprehensive documentation. Instead, it encourages them to pay attention to customer feedback. This facilitates them in addressing new changes with the original requirements.

Therefore, comprehensive collaboration takes the place of extensive documentation. Regular communication with the team is highly effective; it facilitates the team to identify the needs, requirements, and expectations belonging to the project. As a result, client requirements are shaped along with the development of usable products.

Traditional frameworks are limited. They restrict the customer and don't allow deviation from the requirements listed in the contract. However, the Agile project management is customer-oriented; it keeps them involved throughout the complete process. In this way, you can hit two birds with one stone and foster a strong relationship with the client and are more likely to develop a satisfying product that meets their expectation.

4. Responding to Change Over Adhering to a Plan

The Agile project management promotes change among the team members. It doesn't force them to adhere to inflexible and strict plans or schedules. Traditionally, experts opined that accepting modifications or revisions to the actual requirements consumes a lot of time and money, thus it is better to avoid them.

However, resources can be wasted when you are overly committed to in-depth communication. In other cases, the customers themselves are in two minds; they don't know what they want from the beginning. Their expectations were matured over time. This is why stakeholders don't like the final product made from conventional methodologies, because they were never allowed to give feedback at different project stages.

Moreover, change is inevitable in several industries. The world is increasingly becoming competitive and businesses are relying on innovations to outdo each other.

When a project manager rejects change, sooner or later, their plans are going to be outdated. More worryingly, they will find it hard to satisfy their clients.

The Agile project management imparts an important lesson: change does not come under expense. Instead, it provides important feedback that can help you to enhance and refine your project. The change driven by customer's feedback incorporates much-needed value to the project. In the end, the customer is fully satisfied with the outcome.

PRINCIPLES OF AGILE

According to the Agile Manifesto, these are the principles of Agile.

1. Our highest priority is to satisfy the customer through early and continuous delivery of valuable software.
2. Welcome changing requirements, even late in development. Agile processes harness change for the customer's competitive advantage.
3. Deliver working software frequently, from a couple of weeks to a couple of months, with a preference to the shorter timescale.
4. Businesspeople and developers must work together daily throughout the project.
5. Build projects around motivated individuals. Give them the environment and support they need and trust them to get the job done.
6. The most efficient and effective method of conveying information to and within a development team is face-to-face conversation.

7. Working software is the primary measure of progress.
8. Agile processes promote sustainable development. The sponsors, developers, and users should be able to maintain a constant pace indefinitely.
9. Continuous attention to technical excellence and good design enhances agility.
10. Simplicity – the art of maximizing the amount of work not done – is essential.
11. The best architectures, requirements, and designs emerge from self-organizing teams.
12. At regular intervals, the team reflects on how to become more effective, then tunes and adjusts its behavior accordingly.

CHAPTER 3

AGILE PROJECT MANAGEMENT METHODOLOGIES

Scrum's Three Pillars

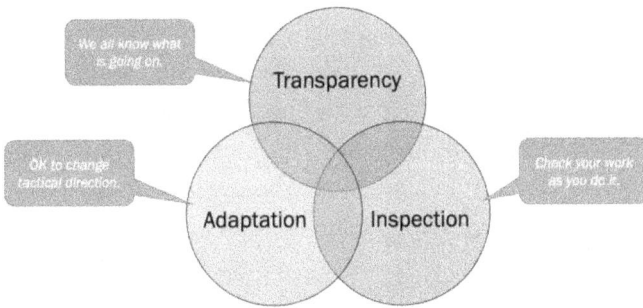

Source: https://scrumorg-website-prod.s3.amazonaws.com/drupal/inline-images/2020-01/3pillarsofempiricism.png

Scrum relies on an empirical approach in order to adapt to the varying customer's requirements. Empiricism allows making decisions according to your recent experience. This approach allows you to improve and learn from your past errors. Here is how Scrum's three-pillar support empirical processes.

Transparency

Transparency in Scrum is done via tools, such as sprint reviews, burndown charts, and product backlog. They employ a cross-functional team to transfer the flow of work. This is beneficial because it offers a clear overview of how the team and work is progressing. As a result, when the team completes a goal, the key performers are visible and receive appreciation for their efforts.

Inspection

Inspection is done by an internal person – anyone from the Scrum team. It can be done for processes, products, continuous improvements, and practices. For instance, the team transparently provides the product to the customer after a Sprint to collect valuable feedback. In case the customer wants revisions during this process, the team customizes the product accordingly and sees it more as an opportunity for collaboration where they can clarify the project requirements with the customer.

Adaptation

Adaptation refers to continuous improvement or the ability to adapt in accordance with inspection's results. The team should daily consider whether their progress is better than the last day. For profit-based companies, this value is shown in the form of profit. Adaptation enables us to run small experiments to find what is working and what is not.

Today, the most popular Agile frameworks are the following.

SCRUM

The Scrum methodology has been primarily created for handling the system development process. It is empirical in nature. It applies the concepts of industrial process control theory against system development. In this way, a new approach is birthed that reinforces productivity, adaptability, and flexibility. The emphasis of Scrum is placed on the functioning of team members – how they create a system flexibly in a rapidly changing environment.

The primary proposition of Scrum rests on this idea that multiple technical and environment variables, such as resources, timeframe, requirements, and technology, cannot stay the same throughout the process. Their evolving nature makes the development process complex and unpredictable. Therefore, the systems development process needs enough flexibility to adapt to the changes. This produces a system that is useful after delivery.

There are three phases in Scrum. In comparison to other project management methodologies, such as spiral, iterative, or waterfall, these three phases are considerably different. Let's review them.

Pre-Game Phase

The pre-game phase is divided into two sub-phases: Planning and Architecture. Planning defines the system that is currently in the development stage. The architecture and high-level design of the system is planned in the architecture phase. Here's a breakdown

Planning

The first step of planning is to create the backlog. It comprises of essential properties that must be implemented in the development process. This responsibility of this sub-phase is assigned to the product owner. They are based on the information from the market situation, clients, and competition requirements. They are also aware of the properties or functions that are needed the most by the product. Other aspects that are discussed in this stage include the number and functionality of release, the delivery date, necessary tools, project team, and structure, list of packets for backlog items, selection (the most important releases) risk control, and release cost. Overall, this Scrum phase is wide-ranging for the new product. If you have an existing system that requires enhancement with some features, then this phase can provide a brief analysis.

Architecture

Planning is followed by the system architecture. The team evaluates the backlog, considers changes that can be made to incorporate new properties, and design the implementation process. In some cases, there's a requirement to make some changes, learn some artificial knowledge, refine the old product, or solve issues that appear during the process. There are also review meetings at the end where teams share information, discuss problems and progress, and reassign changes accordingly.

Development Phase

The development phase is also known as the game phase. This is the Agile component of Scrum methodology. It is considered as a 'black box' of Scrum because this is where the unpredictability factors come in.

Sprint is another name that is used to refer to this phase. It is iterative in nature. Usually, it takes 1-2 weeks (can extend to 4 weeks), and the duration remains similar for all the cycles. However, the time required for each sprint can vary in certain scenarios. This phase is made of four steps:

✓ The team performs an analysis of the product's current situation and takes some key decisions.
✓ Wrap-up closing packets.
✓ Review meetings are arranged to present progress, add new backlog items, resolve issues, and add risk review.
✓ Consolidate the information that was collected from the review into packets.

Post-Game Phase

The release's closure is held by the post-game phase.

Scrum is a proven method for attaining software agility. It uses short sprints to run an iterative cycle until the relevant work items reach completion, finish the deadline, or the budget runs low.

It is vastly different from the conventional waterfall method that readjusts the project scope upfront. It requires a comprehensive formation of documentation related to requirements, analysis, and other aspects. Meanwhile, the project's development can't be launch until the documentation is created. Budget overruns and delays are more common in the waterfall. The inability to highlight the feature set can cause the development of low-quality products. They are overstuffed with features that weren't needed by the client.

Activities in Scrum

Sprint is the main activity of Scrum. It is a time-boxed iteration that can last for anywhere between one to four weeks.

Sprint Planning Meeting

A planning meeting is held at the start of each sprint. It becomes the basis of discussion on what work must be done. The team and product owner review the product backlog and discuss the highest-priority items. Members determine the number of times they can commit. Next, they produce a sprint backlog that comprises of the tasks that are to be completed throughout the sprint.

A product backlog may represent months or weeks of work and it may not be feasible to complete it in a short, single sprint. The ScrumMaster, product owner, and the development team perform sprint planning. They assess the most critical subset of backlog items so the next sprint can be built.

The development team and product owner conform to a sprint goal. It defines what the next sprint is expected to achieve. The development team uses this goal to perform a review of the product backlog. They assess high-priority items that are realistically possible to be accomplished in the next sprint provided work is done at a sustainable pace.

It's a common practice for development teams to split up each targeted feature into a set of tasks. When the relevant product backlog items are combined with these tasks, another backlog is formed known as the sprint backlog.

The development team follows up by providing an estimate (quantified in hours) about how time is needed to accomplish each task.

Daily Scrum

During the sprint, the team members are obliged to share their work details of the previous day on a daily basis. They also explain what is planned for the day and inform the team of any impediments or blockers that will hinder production. These dialing arrangements are key to synchronizing the work done by the team members when they carry out a discussion regarding the sprint's work. These meetings can't go any longer than 15 minutes. It is very important to timebox this daily event.

A standard workflow to perform the daily scrum is one in which the ScrumMaster leads the session and team members answer three questions to help other members: These questions are:

- What was accomplished during the last daily scrum?
- What work will be done on the next daily scrum

- What are the impediments or obstacles that are halting progress?

When these questions are answered, the team gets to know the big picture of what is being done. The daily scrum is crucial because it assists the development team to handle the flexible, rapid workflow of a standard sprint.

Sprint Review

The team showcases the complete functionality at the end of a sprint. A sprint's end has two additional inspect-and-adapt activities. The first one is known as the sprint review. This activity's objective is to examine and adapt the product that is being built. Another thing that is important for the meeting is the conversation that is done between the participants – including the stakeholders, Scrum team, customers, sponsors, and interested members from other teams. The conversation mainly reviews the recently completed features in the context of the overall effort in development.

A review is successful when it creates a bidirectional information flow. Those who are not part of the Scrum team can pick up quickly and guide the direction of the development effort.

Sprint Retrospective

The team engages in retrospective meetings to contemplate the end of the sprint and detect those opportunities that can enhance the new sprint. It is the second inspect-and-adapt activity that occurs at the end of the sprint. While the sprint review is focused on the product, this part places emphasis on the process. The Scrum Master, development team, and product owner communicate during the sprint retrospective to see what works and what does not. Discussion is also done on the relevant technical practices that should be adopted.

When the sprint retrospective comes to an end, the Scrum team is done with identifying and committing to process improvement options that are expected to be done by the Scrum team in the upcoming sprint.

The completion of sprint retrospective is followed by the repetition of the whole cycle, beginning from the upcoming sprint planning session.

Roles of Scrum

Scrum contains three critical roles.

Product Owner

The role of customer proxy is played by the product owner. They are tasked to promote the stakeholders' interest and make sure that priority is given to the product backlog. They are responsible to maximize the return on ROI for which they identify product features, convert them into a prioritized list, and decide what the leading item for the upcoming sprint is, and continue to reprioritize and refine the list. A product owner is also responsible for the profit and loss if it's a commercial product. The responsibilities of a product owner are listed below.

- Possesses the product backlog and writes acceptance criteria and user stories.

- Need to prioritize the product backlog and decide the content and release date.
- Accepts or reject any item in the product backlog.
- Carries the authority to terminate the sprint if they conclude that its goal is redundant.
- Carries the responsibility of the product's ROI.

ScrumMaster

The ScrumMaster carries the responsibility to handle the Scrum. A ScrumMaster is considerably different from a conventional project manager. For example, they don't direct the team daily with project-based instructions. An important part of this role is to eliminate hurdles that stop an activity or slow down the team. The ScrumMaster is responsible for the following:

- Document and eliminates impediments from the team to ensure that the team can concentrate and adhere to scrum practices.
- Encourage and demand the development team to be self-organized.
- Enable coordination between different roles and functions, tackle any resource problem and non-compliance of scrum practices.
- Protect the team from internal and external distractions.

Development Team

The development team is a cross-functional group that is tasked to develop the product. It is composed of 5-9 members. This team can include UI designers, programmers, system analysts, software engineers, QA experts, testers, and system administrators. The responsibilities of the development team are listed below:

- Builds the product according to the wishes of the product owner. For instance, it can be a website.
- Carries the required skill set to deliver a shippable product after each sprint.
- Makes decisions on the number of items that are needed to be built in a sprint.
- Owns the responsibility as a self-organized and cross-functional team to develop, test, and release the product increment.

Artifacts in Scrum

There are not many artifacts in Scrum since it is more focused on delivering value-oriented software. Here are the chief artifacts in Scrum:

Product Backlog

It is a list of features that must be integrated into the project. The product backlog is the single source of requirements for any revisions that need to be done to the product. It contains requirements, functions, features, fixes, and enhancements as changes that are required to be completed for future releases. These items can have attributions of order, description, value, and estimate. These items are also known as user stories.

A product backlog keeps on changing. The first version comprises of the initial requirements. It gets developed as a product. Similarly, its intended environment evolves too. The product backlog becomes more exhaustive and larger as the product is being used and generates value. Constant modifications in the market conditions, technology, and business requirements force the backlog to change continually. Therefore, it is also known as a live artifact.

Sprint Backlog

It is a list of tasks that have a higher priority than others. The sprint backlog is essentially a set of items from the product backlog that are chosen for the sprint. The team uses this artifact to forecast what functionality can be made available in the upcoming increment and the work required to deliver that functionality.

The sprint backlog contains detail which can be easily understood by the team, but they need to track it in the daily scrum. The team continues to revise this backlog throughout the sprint's lifecycle.

When new work comes, the team pushes it to the sprint backlog. While the work is being performed, the team updates the estimated remaining work. If any element of the backlog is found to be unnecessary, it is removed right away.

Burndown charts

A burndown chart is a type of graphical representation of the remaining work versus time.

These charts help to estimate the remaining amount of work in a sprint. The team monitors this work for daily scrums to make projections on whether the sprint goal is achievable. The team can streamline its progress more effectively after tracking the remaining work.

The remaining work from the sprint backlog can be summed at any point in the time. This helps to find out the possibility of accomplishing sprint goals.

Usually, the remaining work is represented on the vertical axis while the time is shown on the horizontal axis. It helps to:

- Monitor the project scope.
- Tracks the team's velocity.
- Keep the team on schedule.
- Compare the team progression against the planned work.

RAPID APPLICATION DEVELOPMENT

The main advantage of a RAD approach is quick project turnaround, which makes it appealing for software developers who are part of a fast-paced environment. The speed of the approach comes from its emphasis to minimize the planning stage and expand the prototype development.

RAD empowers stakeholders and project managers to evaluate progress in an accurate manner. They engage in real-time communication on changes or evolving issues. This increases the speed of development, makes communication more effective, and incorporates efficiency to the whole project.

Phases of RAD

Generally, there are four RAD phases.

Requirements Planning

The underlying theme of this phase is similar to the project scope meeting. Even though the planning phase is cut down, it remains an important step for the project's success.

Throughout this stage, team members, developers, and clients chat among themselves to figure out the following aspects.

✓ Project goals
✓ Expectations from the project
✓ Current and potential problems that require fixing during the build period.

Here are the common activities of this stage:

• Conduct thorough research on the current issue.
• Define the project requirements.
• Get the stakeholder's approval to finalize the requirements.

It's critical that all the members are allowed to view the project goals and expectations. Receiving approach from the relevant stakeholders and developers can reduce miscommunications to a considerable extent.

User Design

After the project scope is realized, you can construct the user design via different prototype iterations. This is the core part of the RAD methodology and makes it stand out from other methodologies. In this phase, clients work closely with developers to address requirements at every step of the design process. It bears a resemblance to customizable software development and allows users to perform testing for products at suitable stages, in a bid to address expectations.

During the User Design phase bugs are resolved through an iterative cycle. The developer creates a prototype, allows it to get tested by the user, and hold discussions on what works and what does not.

Rapid Construction

This stage picks up the beta systems and prototypes collected in the design phase and transforms them into a working model.

Since the iterative design phase allowed resolving most of the changes and issues, developers can build the final working model in a lesser amount of time than the time required in conventional projects. This phase is split up into the following steps:

- Preparation for rapid construction
- Program and application development
- Coding
- Testing (e.g., unit, integration, and system)

During this phase, the team of developers, testers, and other critical roles collaborate to ensure that everything works smoothly, and the final outcome can satisfy the objective and expectations of the client.

Also known as the implementation phase, this is the stage where the finished product is prepared for launch. It comprises of testing, data conversion, user training, and changeover to the new system. The final changes are approved as the clients and coders examine the system for bugs.

KANBAN

Kanban is a framework that is used for the implementation of Agile software delivery. It needs full transparency of work and real-time communication. A Kanban board is used to represent work items, letting team members observe the state of different pieces of work items whenever they want it.

Kanban allows developers to use JIT (just in time) principles and match work in progress to the capacity of the team. In this way, teams benefit from clearer focus, faster output, flexible planning options, and transparency across the development cycle.

Despite the origins of the framework dating back to 1940s, its core principles have been applicable and timeless for a wide range of industries. Software developers have particularly found it to be effective. A major reason behind this is that development teams can start implementing it with almost no overhead after they have become familiar with its principles. On the factory floor, Kanban implementation requires adjustments to physical processes and adding substantial materials. On the other hand, software developers don't need anything to start over with it. There are boards and cards; you can use the virtual ones.

Boards in Kanban

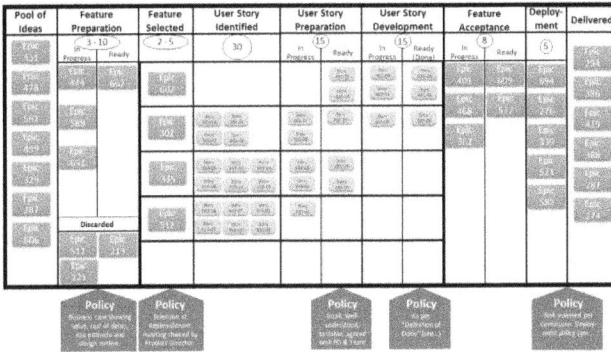

The working of Kanban teams is based around a tool known as a Kanban board. It visualizes work and optimizes the workflow of a team. Although physical boards are widely used, virtual boards are an integral cog of any Agile software development methodology. They are beneficial because of easier collaboration, traceability, and accessibility from different locations.

No matter what the type of a board is, they are used for visualizing your team's work, standardize the workflow, and identify and resolve any dependency or blocker. Typically, a Kanban board operates on a workflow comprising of three steps: To Do, In Progress, and Done.

However, you can map it to comply with a unique process based on your team's objectives, structure, and size.

Cards in Kanban

Cards are used to represent work on the Kanban board. It facilitates team members in tracking the work progress via its workflow with enhanced visualizations. These cards contain critical pieces of information related to a specific work item, providing maximum visibility to the entire team so they know the following:

- Who has been assigned that item of work?
- What has been done so far on the item of work?
- How long is that item of work going to take?

Virtual Kanban boards also contain cards that show screenshots and similar technical details that are useful for the assignee. Kanban is very similar to Scrum up to a certain extent. But both functions are based on different concepts. Here is how Kanban is different:

- Kanban is run through continuous flow – unlike Scrum's fixed length sprints.
- The key metric in Kanban is cycle time, whereas Scrum has velocity.
- Scrum discourages making changes during the sprint, but Kanban embraces changes at all times.
- There are no existing roles in Kanban like the Scrum Master in Scrum.
- The release of Scrum is dependent on the product owner, while Kanban uses continuous delivery or relies on the team for releases.

SCRUMBAN

As the name suggests, Scrumban is an Agile hybrid of Scrum and Kanban. It was designed to help software development teams transition from Scrum to Kanban. As a hybrid Agile methodology, it combines the best of both worlds and is suitable for development and product projects.

Scrumban adopts the prescriptive essence of Scrum that works on the basis of the Agile framework and extract Kanban's key process of improvement. This empowers teams to optimize its processes regularly.

Some teams that migrated to Scrumban often desired to put an end to their work in sprints. They found Kanban more feasible due to its pull-based system. Hence, this led to the emergence of a hybrid of both frameworks. It extracts the best features of both frameworks, which is why Scrumban teams have a lot of room for flexibility when it comes to adapting to changes.

Influence of Scrum and Kanban on Scrumban

The excellence of Scrumban is derived from its integration of the Scrum's defined structure to Kanban's fluid workflows. Here's how Scrumban depends on them.

Scrum Influence

Scrumban takes decision-making from Scrum, such as determine the estimated amount of work that can be done in a sprint and prioritizing and switching to the most critical part. However, this work is finished only when the required analysis is executed; it is part of the Scrum definition of ready. The ready list helps with organizing tasks between the doing stage and backlog.

Kanban Influence

Scrumban taps into Kanban to enhance the process and optimize the visualization of workflow. Scrumban adopts Kanban's pull system, providing a continuous flow. This means that tasks are arranged in the doing column as soon as the team is ready for execution.

Kanban also improves Scrumban by restricting the number of items that are in progress at a time. This builds up focus on certain tasks and boosts productivity. As opposed to Scrum, there are no individual roles in Kanban, making it more flexible.

Kanban also inherits JIT from Kanban; it produces shorter lead times for iteration planning estimates. Moreover, buffers and flow diagrams are used to detect weaknesses in the processes. This shows areas that can become better with improvement and decreases bottlenecks.

EXTREME PROGRAMMING

Extreme Programming is designed to enhance software quality and its capability to adapt to evolving customer needs. Like other Agile methods, Extreme Programming is targeted to offer frequent and iterative small releases in a project. It enables customers and team members to inspect and review the progress of a project across the whole software development lifecycle.

XP Values

There are five foundation values that set the foundation of the XP paradigm.

Communication

Software development is a team sport that depends on communication to spread knowledge and information between all the members of a team. XP places emphasis on the significance of a suitable form of communication – face-to-face discussion, assisted by a drawing mechanism, such as a whiteboard for the best results.

Simplicity

Simplicity is all about finding out the simplest solution that will work. The aim is to perform only the necessary tasks like keeping a simple design for a system. This makes it easy to revise, support, and maintain. Simplicity also ensures that you only work on the requirements that are known, rather than attempting to predict anything and add anything by yourself.

Feedback

Teams can find areas for improvement and readjust their practices through constant feedback related to their previous efforts. Feedback also lends support to a simple design. Your team builds something, collects feedback on areas such as design and implementation, and revises the product accordingly.

Courage

It is officially defined as "effective action in the face of fear". It indicates an affinity for action based on other principles. In this way, the outcomes don't pose any threat to the team. Courage is essential when it comes to pointing your finger at organizational issues that hamper the effectiveness of your team. Courage helps you put an end to something that was always going to fail and adopt a better solution. You also need it to embrace feedback and follow it with an action, even if it is tough to acknowledge.

Respect

Your team members must extend respect to each other if they want to improve communication for the projects. They need to offer and accept feedback that improves your relationship and collaborate to come up with designs and solutions.

DYNAMIC SOFTWARE DEVELOPMENT MODEL

As Agile comes of age, DSDM has attracted a great deal of attraction. It is especially popular among organizations that want to exert greater control during their Agile use without having the ideal Agile environment.

DSDM deals with the requirements of complex project scenarios – which consist of multiple teams distributed across various time zones and countries. It also works for simpler product development where teams are co-located.

DSDM is a framework that is composed of eight principles, roles and responsibilities, a lifecycle and products, and many best practice techniques. It promotes a philosophy of providing benefits that are strategically aligned to the organizational benefits as early as possible so the organization can earn the best ROI.

DSDM helps to address common issues recurring in projects, such as cost overruns, late delivery, and the lack of suitability of the final deliverable. To address these concerns, DSDM produces an Agile environment which is flexible, collaborative, and is highly dedicated to hit deadlines and maintain a suitable level of rigor and quality.

DSDM also makes stakeholders such as the business representatives participate during an incremental and iterative lifecycle. Each member of the team is assigned a clear role and responsibility. They must collaborate via time-boxes to make sure that the project keeps meeting the deadlines.

Principles of DSDM

DSDM is made of the following principles.

Active user involvement is imperative.

The emphasis of DSDM on the system's business purpose ensures that the end-user is involved throughout the development lifecycle. This is required because the system attributes that must align well with its purpose cannot be perceived properly in the project's early stages; hence they are stopped from committing to a detailed specification. The only method to make suitable in-depth decisions is to let users participate throughout the project.

Empower the DSDM teams

This doesn't, in any way, give free rein to the team. Instead, it calls for the team to gain authority and take the majority of the day-to-day decisions as the project continues to expand. Active user involvement can ensure that this delegation of power allows the team to perform faster and steadily towards the delivery of the final product. But when an issue such as cost overruns emerges where the decision-making capability does not fall under the team's authority, DSDM acknowledges that such decisions should be taken by the right authority outside of the team.

The focus is on frequent delivery of products.

This means that you should measure the project progress in terms of tangible products, instead of only assessing activity. Understand that the "delivery of products" is not only pointing towards a working system's incremental delivery for an end-user. It also considers any work product that is created when the project moves ahead— the product could be a design document, a throwaway prototype, or a specification. And the delivery is expected to be executed by the project team. DSDM recommends that as the project goes ahead, it should continue to create artifacts that show continual progress.

Fitness for business purpose is the essential criterion for acceptance of deliverables.

Here you can observe a practical manifestation of the DSDM's philosophy that defining details requirements upfront doesn't help your project. Rather than the satisfaction of requirements, prioritize fitness for purpose and involve users consistently. DSDM pays attention to the end user as the sole entity who has a say on whether the system is acceptable while it is being modified.

Iterative and incremental development is important for an accurate business solution.

Incremental development is excellent insurance when anything in the project goes wrong, especially in an environment where you can't predict the end result in complete detail. Here, incremental development is a trial and error workflow where the user gets the new increment and this user reserves the right to validate or invalidate the direction of a project team. It is presumed that you don't know what the most direct path to the end product is. Therefore, DSDM makes use of continuous checks and corrects the path so the project ends on a satisfactory note.

All changes during development are reversible.

If it is accepted that the project is an exercise of trial and error, then we are likely to receive errors throughout the development lifecycle. This principle authorizes us to remove faulty work when deemed necessary. Although you keep might try to repair the issue, but in some scenarios, discarding some work and coming up with a new solution is the most efficient route.

Requirements are baselined at a high level

This principle underlines the departure of DSDM from other Agile methods. DSDM notes the significance of direction and scope to a project. Stakeholders freeze some requirements at some level to lay the foundation of a stable basis for the work of a team.

Incorporating testing throughout the lifecycle

Testing does not appear as a step in the DSDM lifecycle as it binds members to adopt a strong-quality consciousness. Each task should have a suitable validation or verification step, such as a test or a review by a user or a team member. This principle coordinates with other principles like 1, 4, and 5 to regularly assess the progress of a project for a goal so it can become fit for a business purpose.

A cooperative and collaborative approach is mandatory between all the stakeholders

The sum of the first eight principles paves the way for the last principle. When all the stakeholders embrace DSDM and its roles, the principles of 1-8 can be implemented successfully. If any stakeholder doesn't agree, DSDM ceases to work in that environment.

CRYSTAL

In 1991, IBM conveyed to Alistair Cockburn about a need to create a methodology that can work with object-oriented projects. Cockburn realized that it was going to be hard, especially since he did not know much about project methodologies. To find a viable solution, he set out to interview project teams and collected opinions on their projects.

After Cockburn was done, he concluded that successful teams shared similar techniques and methods; even when they did not use any specific project methodology. This meant that the added value came from aspects such as close communication, access to users, morale, and others – ones that cannot be found in any specific methodology. He used this research to create a comprehensive methodology, crystal.

Crystal is an Agile approach that is focused mainly on people, especially how they interact while working on a project, rather than highlighting processes and tools. Alistair Cockburn opined that the skill sets, talents, and communication skills of people have the most impact on a project's outcome. The crystal approach is centered on two assumptions:

- Every project is unique and needs specific methods.
- Teams can streamline their processes and gain greater optimization.

In Crystal, product development is a sort of game that must stimulate everyone so they can produce great ideas, become creative, and interact with each other. Such a strategy answers questions such as "do we have our goals aligned as a team?"

Family

The properties of a project depend on the total number of people working on it as well as the project's criticality level. Although small teams can manage and build the product without much paperwork and status reporting, bigger teams need to work with a higher number of communication artifacts for large-scale projects. Hence, the more people on a team indicate its criticality and signal the need for a more complex approach. Therefore, Crystal is a family of multiple methodologies.

There are three dimensions that form your approach for a project.

- Team size
- Criticality
- Priority of the project

Generally, crystal methods are characterized by colors.

- A team of 50-100 people adopts Red methodology.
- A team of 20-50 people adopts Orange methodology.
- A team of 10-20 people adopts Yellow methodology.
- A team of 8 or fewer people adopts the Clear methodology.

Crystal is considered among the most flexible Agile frameworks because it revolves around people – not any specific tool or processes. Therefore, it is a good tool for organizations that want to empower their teams with greater freedom. It is important to note that Crystal prioritizes direct team collaboration but de-emphasizes the significance of reporting and documentation.

CRYSTAL CLEAR

As mentioned before, crystal clear is used for small teams. The group size is important because smaller teams help to pick up a methodology that is suitable for the project. This methodology prioritizes people over process. Crystal clear is preferred when your team is working on non-critical projects.

Cycle Process

Typically, a crystal-clear process comprises of 6 cycles:

- Project Cycle – The project is followed by another project. The project cycle is made of three parts: preparation, two or more delivery cycles, and a competition ritual.
- Delivery Cycle – Comprises readjusting the software's release plan. Tested integrated code is used to produce one or more iterations, which are delivered to real users.
- Iteration – Made of three major parts: iterative planning, cycle's day and integration activities, and the project's completion ritual.
- Working day/week – Selecting the week or day as a unit of cycle time is based on the project team and format. It can include reporting meetings of team leaders, weekly meetings of departments, and, brown-bag seminars.
- Integration period – Consists of system development, integration, and testing. Sometimes, the assembly-testing process continues unstopped in a separate machine. A shorter integration cycle is desirable.

- Development – Writing and testing code. A team member works on a small task, creates a solution with testing, and adds it to the configuration. It can take a few minutes to several days.

Principles of Crystal Clear

Crystal Clear works on the basis of 7 principles.

Frequent Delivery

It is important to deliver software to clients frequently. It can be sent delivered daily, weekly, or monthly.

Reflective Improvement

Crystal Clear is not too prescriptive. It transfers a lot of things to the team so they can think and agree after discussing it among themselves. The team coordinates to determine which idea creates better results and use these insights for future practices.

Osmotic Communication

The team should work in the same workspace. In this way, they can learn from each other.

Personal Safety

Members should embrace and approach the ideas of each without reprimanding or ridiculing each other. Mutual trust needs to be developed within the team so they can resolve issues quickly and enhance performance.

Focus

Project leaders need to assign priorities to each project and explain them to the team in detail. Team members should get enough time and space to focus on their tasks without being interrupted.

Easy Access to Expert Users

Developers should roll out their products and get feedback from users. Continuously doing this can enhance the quality of products.

Technical Environment

The project needs to be handled in an appropriate environment. It should be equipped with effective configuration management, frequent integration, and automated tests.

ADAPTIVE SOFTWARE DEVELOPMENT

Adaptive software development is borrowed from RAD practices to a certain extent.

Phases of ASD

ASD is cyclical. The phase names reflect the unpredictability of the complex systems. These phases include:

Speculation

Speculation comprises of risk-driven adaptive cycle planning and project initiation. Developers utilize this phase to determine the exact requirements and nature of the software. The phase depends on user and bug reports.

Adaptive Cycle Planning

- Figure out the project time-box.
- Measure the optimal count of time-box for each.
- Create an objective statement for each time-box.
- Assign components and technology to cycle.
- Create a project task list.

Project Initiation

- Mention the project objectives, constraints, and mission.
- Assess the guideline parameters of the project.
- Collect system requirements.
- Organize the project.
- Estimate project scope and size.

Collaboration

This is the hard part about ASD as you need to motivate your workers. Although it promotes teamwork and communication, it emphasizes that individual creativity is crucial for creative thinking. People who work together should trust each to:

- Communicate issues to determine a feasible solution.
- Work as hard as possible.
- Offer constructive criticism.
- Help without any feelings of animosity or resentment.

Learning

This phase contains a review and the final QA. It releases the latest software version to users. In this way, user and bug reports are produced that are used in the project's first phase.

Quality Review

Learning activities represent the end of each cycle. Project team is required to work on planning at the beginning of the cycle. ASD teams learn on the basis of the following:

✓ Technical Reviews
✓ Focus Groups
✓ Project postmortems

Final QA and Release

Finally, hand off the product to the end-user. Consolidate all the information on the product and give it to the customer, followed by the disbandment of the project team.

LEAN

Lean project management methodology improves processes and reduces waste. It works to enhance the efficiency of all the processes in an organization.

Principles of Lean

Lean consists of the following principles.

Value

The first principle focuses on understanding a service or product's value for the customer. The amount a customer wants to pay for a product/service is related to how much they value it. Therefore, it is important to understand a product's value.

The value stream is the total sequence of activities that deliver an end-product with a mutually agreed value. Map the value stream refers to visualization methods, such as spaghetti diagrams, flowcharts, or Kanban to show this flow.

Value Stream

The final goal of value stream mapping is the optimization and preservation of flow.

Flow

After waste is eliminated, you should aim for a smooth project flow. It should proceed without any delays and interruptions.

Pull

Pull needs a high flexibility level. Managers should take decisions for a course of action after customer orders or controls it. This consists of schedules or forecasts to push work.

Some of the tools used in Lean project management include:

- Root Cause Analysis (RCA) to determine and remove issues that create troubles.
- Customer feedback to explain the points of improvement.
- Gantt chart to track progress.
- Statistical process control (SPC) to assess performance.

FEATURE-DRIVEN DEVELOPMENT

Feature-Driven Development is a framework that methodizes software development on making progress on features. These features are not always product features. If you have worked with user stories in Scrum, then they are closer to user stories in Scrum.

Iteration Zero

Iteration zero is a short period in which a team organizes what is required to begin delivering on the client-oriented functionality in upcoming iterations.

In FDD, a project is based on five processes. The first three processes are similar to general iteration zero activities. Let's go over the brief overview of FDD processes.

Process 1:

In FDD, the object model building activity is not as long or drawn-out as it is in other Agile methodologies. It is executed via CASE tools. There is no formatting of the model into a larger document nor do they send it to the developers without any due consideration.

On the contrary, in FDD, creating an initial object model is a collaborative, highly iterative, and intense activity that involves development and domain members where a chief architect guides the team as an object modeler.

This process mentions the quality checks and tasks required for completing the work. Although not necessary, the object model is often created with the help of color technique taken from the modeling of Peter Coad.

The concept emphasizes on both development and domain team members to get a shared perspective so they can analyze and understand the problem domain. Everyone needs to have a grip on the problem domain concepts, interactions, and relationships. This ensures that the team collaborates and forms a shared vocabulary. Up to this point, the object model is geared towards breadth rather than depth. Depth develops over time during the project's lifetime. The results of this is a living artifact in the form of a model.

Process 2:

You might think that FDD is driven by the object model because of building it in the first activity. However, it is very similar to Extreme Programming or Scrum when it comes to being driven by requirements. Features or client's desirable requirements take the project forward while the model acts as a guiding force. A feature is defined by the following expression: <action> <result>

<object>. These features are small, so they take 3 days on average and 10 days at most for implementation.

FDD creates a feature list which works with a three-level hierarchy to arrange features. This is helpful for larger projects and teams. It allows them to handle a larger number of items that are usually specified on an FDD's features list.

The team defines the hierarchy's upper levels by extracting a group of domain subject areas. They are gathered from the problem domain's high-level breakdown. Next, the team specifies business activities for each area and adds individual features accordingly. Therefore, you will observe that the feature list includes features that originate from activities.

Process 3:

The last process of FDD revolves around creating and assigning initial schedule and responsibilities. Activities-filled feature sets are sequenced by the planning team based on business value. The chief programmer is responsible to develop these feature sets. Hence, when this process is completed, they are assigned a subset of the features list. It's more like the features' virtual inbox which they can incorporate.

The order of feature sets might be adjusted by the planning team. They assess it in terms of dependencies and technical risks.

FDD stays clear of conventional Agile thinking. It does this by not taking the source code's collective ownership.

It delegates each developer to take responsibility of specific classes.

There can be certain problems when it comes to assigning ownership of the code. For instance, XP prefers collective ownership to resolve issues. On the other hand, an FDD doesn't allow two developers to revise code as per their wishes. It adopts a different approach for code ownership.

Do note that in FDD, class ownership is not exclusivity; it is responsibility. A class owner can approve a change in their class, which is done by a developer. This is different from extreme programming. Here, the class owner knows and approves of the change and must check whether the change was performed properly. It can become hard to maintain complete ownership of code as the size of the team increases.

The structure of FDD planning is similar to other Agile frameworks. The planning team assesses and changes the order of classes to developers and feature sets to chief programmers when deemed necessary. Additionally, they wait for other classes to come out and thus don't always appoint owners to the domain classes.

AGILE UNIFIED PROCESS

Agile Unified Process is a simpler form of rational unified process (RUP). It entails a straightforward approach for creating enterprise systems by applying Agile concepts and techniques while at the same time it borrows from the RUP. Usually, Agile techniques that are applied to AUP include database refactoring, Agile change management,

Agile Model Driven Development (AMDD), and test-driven development (TDD for boosting productivity.

Serial Nature

The AUP exhibits a serial nature in the following phases.

1. Inception – The objective is to understand the project's initial scope, potential system architecture, and acquire stakeholder trust, leading to initial project funding.
2. Elaboration – The objective is to prove the system's architecture.
3. Construction – The objective is to create a working system on an incremental, continuous basis. It must meet the project needs in accordance with priority.
4. Transition – The objective is to go ahead with validation and then deploy the system in the appropriate productive environment.

Iterative Approach

The AUP follows an iterative approach when it comes to disciplines. It specifies the activities that team members must perform to validate, build, and deliver working a system that addresses the stakeholders' requirements. These disciplines are:

- Model – The objective is to get the hang of the organization's business aspect, understand the project's problem domain, and find the right solution for it.
- Test – The objective is to ensure quality by performing an objective evaluation. It consists of

identifying defects, performing system validation as agreed, and verifying that requirements were addressed.

- Deployment – The objective is to create a plan for the system's delivery and initiate work on the plan, so the system becomes available to end-users.
- Configuration Management – The objective is to oversee the project artifacts' access. It consists of not only monitoring artifact versions regularly, but also directing and handling changes to them.
- Project Management – The objective is to control the project activities. It consists of handling risks, managing people, and work alongside the systems and people outside the project's scope to ensure that the project gets delivered on schedule without exceeding the budget.
- Environment – The objective is to provide support to the remaining effort. It makes sure that the right guidance, process, and tools are made available to the team.

CHAPTER 4

WHY SHOULD ORGANIZATIONS CHOOSE AGILE?

HURDLES FACED BY ORGANIZATIONS IMPLEMENTING AGILE

Agile development methodologies come from real-life experiences of software engineers. These developers felt bogged down by the limitations of conventional waterfall methodology. The Agile approach works well as a direct response to the challenges linked with conventional software design, with respect to specific processes and the underlying philosophy. Before we learn about what makes Agile so beneficial, here are some of the biggest challenges that organizations face during the implementation of Agile processes.

1. Company Culture

It's tough to reform how people plan and function. The beliefs and habits of a large company are quite deep-rooted. Usually, people attempt to resist change. In cases, when Agile transformation challenges them, they come with different excuses.

Offering a room for an adjustment suggests that you're accepting that you are not following the best practice. Or worse, it can be problematic for the established values of a person.

The management is required to deal with desired output. Whether you are looking to increase the process' predictability or achieving a quicker time to promote your people, your people will be able to adopt the change if they believe and understand the desired results of Agile.

2. Lack of Team Ownership

The objective of Agile is to help members take complete responsibility for their work's ownership. They also don't have to rely on others. When this is done effectively, it needs the project manager to expand communication among team members and encourage engagement with the project.

With Agile, you increase ownership of the team members. They would have to assess and determine how to find solutions whenever an issue emerges, which costs significant delays. It misspends critical time, waiting for approvals to complete the tasks.

3. Lack of Dedicated Cross-Functional Teams

The language used in developing the principles and manifestos of Agile refers to the Agile team members as the developers. Because of this, several people think that developers are needed for an Agile team. The term developer, which is utilized in the manifesto's guidelines, refers to service or product developer. This describes the cross-functional role, which is needed for assisting the team that delivers the project.

Agile cross-functional teams work incrementally and iteratively, expanding opportunities for feedback. It ensures that a working product is always available. Despite the fact that the idea of cross-functional teams is relatively old, companies find it hard to adapt to it.

4. Poor Communication

Communication is essential in Agile. Team members need to communicate properly and effectively so the project goes well. The organization needs to offer adequate communications channels, especially for distributed teams. Usually, teams are co-located in Agile organizations. Working in the same workspace enables quick information flow and generates timely feedback. Co-located teams also help you to take advantage of osmotic communication.

On the other hand, for distributed teams in which team members meet in different offices, communication is quite complex and inefficient. In other scenarios, various teams meet in different time zones. For both cases, you need to hire the right job person who has terrific communication skills to reduce miscommunication.

BENEFITS OF ADOPTING AGILE

There are numerous benefits of using Agile for your project management. Agile project methodology allows the team to handle work more effectively and efficiently while offering the best quality product on a limited budget. Agile teams coordinate nicely as a unit and responds well to the inevitable revisions that exists typically in majority of the projects. Here are the benefits of Agile.

1. Stakeholder Engagement

Agile offers a wide range of opportunities to the stakeholder. Similarly, it boosts team engagement throughout the Sprint. When the client is involved in all the project steps, there's enhanced collaboration between the project team and the client. Creating a working system frequently boosts the trust of the stakeholders in the team's ability and they are confident that the team can develop quality software and motivate them to engage more in the project.

2. Transparency

An Agile methodology offers a distinct chance to clients to take an active part throughout the project lifecycle – from iterating planning and review sessions to software builds. The clients also need to accept that they are overseeing a work in progress in return for transparency.

The lack of a visible process makes it challenging to adapt in accordance with newer changes and measure performance indicators. Therefore, Agile projects are known for transparency in their workflows. It enables you to identify workflow issues, unify your team, get them on the same page, and tackle changes with greater success.

For example, the Kanban board can add more transparency to your project's lifecycle. It divides your larger initiatives into smaller tasks (cards), breaks down your work process into multiple phases, develops independent workflows, creates explicit policies, and provides an overview of how your team members contribute when it comes to different tasks.

3. Predictable Delivery

The time-box, regular Sprints, delivered within four weeks allow you to provide new features rapidly and frequently, creating a greater level of predictability. In this way, you can decide whether you need to release the product or perform beta testing of the software earlier than scheduled, provided there is enough business value.

4. Costs and Schedule

Since each Sprint comprises of a fixed duration, the cost is predictable and restricted to work that the team performs for the relevant time-box. Along with the estimations given to the client before each Sprint, the client is well-equipped to go through each feature's suitable cost.

5. Enable Change

Although the team is required to monitor the delivery of a product's features for each iteration, you reprioritize and refine the entire product backlog. Plan the changed or new backlog items for the succeeding iteration, offering the possibility to present changes within weeks.

6. Focus on Business Value

The team finds what is necessary to the client's business by asking the client to prioritize features in an order. In this way, they provide the features with higher business value first.

7. Focus on Users

Agile specify product features by using user stories having business-oriented criteria. When only those features are concentrated that represent real-world user needs, each of them is not merely an IT component, it incrementally adds a value. You can also perform your software's beta testing in this way after each Sprint, acquiring useful feedback early in the project and incorporate changes as per the requirements.

8. Boost Quality

When you split up the project in manageable units, the team can focus on high-quality development, collaboration, and testing. The production of frequent builds and proceeding with reviews and testing for each iteration is beneficial. It improves the process of identifying and resolving defects to a great extent.

9. Relevant Metrics

Agile generates accurate and relevant metrics that help with project planning and performance assessment. In conventional project management, metrics are primarily utilized to track the project against schedule and cost. However, one thing that gets overlooked is efficiency.

However, Agile has several embed tools that measures efficiency as well as promotes optimizing performance, producing outcomes, and making data-driven decisions.

For example, when you work towards measuring your team's performance and optimizing your work process, you can use the following metrics in Agile.

- Cycle Time – It shows the time spent on a specific work item.
- Lead Time – It assesses the time taken in processing one work item from the initial customer request to the eventual delivery.
- Throughput – It represents your team's productivity and measures it. It evaluates the amount of finished work at any given time.
- Aging Work in Progress – It tracks how your work in progress evolves over time, especially where it slows down and moves faster for a given process.

For project planning and scheduling, Agile prefers forecasting over gut feelings. The next section will discuss the metrics in detail.

10. Continuous Improvement and Clear Process

Agile implementation produces a clear process where open communication is prioritized as the ideal method for sharing ideas. Along with visualization, this approach decreases the time needed to deliver per message across the team. As a result, understanding of each step is improved for a process. It contributes towards the development of an informed team that is aware of the common goal and what needs to be done to finish it.

Besides, Agile prioritizes continuous improvement. When larger workloads are split into smaller pieces and reach the customer for review, Agile teams receive feedback and refine a product/service by improving its quality over time.

After an agreed-upon time, the end customers receive what they need, but were unable to communicate in the early phases of the project. Furthermore, the knowledge gained by your team throughout the process makes them more experienced and qualified to execute future projects successfully.

MEASURING THE AGILE SUCCESS

Agile success is measured through several metrics. These are standards that help with monitoring a team's productivity for different phases through the Software Development Life Cycle (SDLC). These metrics are important to assess the development process because they allow evaluating project quality.

1. Sprint Burndown Report

The time-bound nature of Sprints makes it necessary to track the progress of tasks periodically. A sprint burndown report is used to monitor completed tasks in a sprint. The parameters of measurements are time and work, represented by the x-axis and y-axis, respectively. The unit of measurement is story points or hours. The team performs forecasting for the workload at the start of a sprint. The target is to finish the workload by the sprint's end.

2. Velocity

Velocity shows the average work done by a team throughout a sprint. The report consists of multiple iterations. The forecast's accuracy relies on the total number of iterations – each iteration boosts the accuracy. The unit of measurement is story points or hours. Velocity evaluates a team's ability to deal with backlogs and evolves over time. Velocity is tracked through consistent performance. The decline of velocity indicates that the team must adjust or fix something within their process.

3. Epic and Release Burndown

Epic and release burndown monitors performance for larger work bodies. Sprints have a lot of epics and versions of work. Therefore, it's necessary to monitor their performance. The whole team needs to know the workflow in the epic and version.

4. Control Chart

The time spent from "in progress" and "complete" status of tasks is represented by the control charts. Their emphasis is on finding how much cycle time is taken by a single issue. Predictable teams are those where teams are consistent with cycle teams. Additionally, higher throughput is generated among teams with short cycle times. Comparing cycle times enhances the flexibility of each process. For example, it can help with discerning the changes quickly when a change occurs. This allows the team to perform the required adjustments.

5. Cumulative Flow Diagram

The cumulative flow diagram (CFD) imbues consistency in a team's workflow. The x-axis and y-axis represent the number of issues and time respectively. A smooth left-to-right pattern indicates an ideal diagram. Uneven flow should be smoothened by the color bands. When the band narrows, it points out that the throughput is greater than the rate of entry. A widened band indicates that your workflow capacity is more than enough; you can move it somewhere else for streamlining the flow.

6. Net Promoter Score

The net promoter score compares the willingness of customers to recommend a service or product to others. It can be anywhere between -100 to 100. A firm's success can be assessed by customer loyalty. For this purpose, you can rely on the Net Promoter Score.

7. Blocked Time

Here, each task is assigned with a blocker sticker. It shows that the assignee can't go ahead with a specific task due to some reason. Once the dependency is addressed, the blocked card is moved to the right on the task board. Compare the duration and number of blocked cards to count the total blockers. Addressing the blockers ensures that you complete the "in progress" tasks swiftly.

8. Quality Intelligence

Quality intelligence is required when you are searching for clarity on software quality. It identifies recent code changes. For instance, it can show new codes that have been developed but are yet to be tested. Sometimes code quality can decline. Quality intelligence addresses this issue and informs the team of whether they need to dedicate more time to testing.

9. Escaped Defects

When bugs accumulate in production, it leads to unanticipated damage. They cause issues and the team must resolve them. Metrics related to escaped defects assist in identifying a bug after a release enters production. The software quality is measured in the raw form.

10. Failed Deployments

Failed deployments allow you to determine the count of total deployments. Furthermore, teams can assess the reliability of a production and testing environment. You can use this metric to decide whether a sprint can enter production or not.

11. Code Coverage

Code coverage determines how many unit tests are covered by the code. This metric can be run for every build. The code coverage is shown in the raw form. It provides a useful overview of progress. However, it does not involve other testing forms. Therefore, high quality is not always represented by high code coverage.

CHOOSING THE RIGHT METHODOLOGY

Agile project management methodologies are trending in the last few years. However, studies reveal that 50% of Agile projects fail due to the incorrect use of the methodology. Choosing the most suitable methodology is challenging. Here are some factors and their sub-factors that play a pivotal role in picking an Agile methodology.

1. Development Team's Skills

The capability and skills of development teams in a specific area is important. Different skill sets differ based on their company and the selected methodology. Sometimes, methodologies require a higher level of programming skills complemented by effective communication skills. Examples include XP.

Communication Skill

The Agile methodology outlines a collaborative approach. As a result of this, the communication skill of the development team is directly linked to the methodology's success. Depending upon the team locations and project size, communication could be either indirect or direct.

Competency

While picking an Agile methodology, it's necessary to determine the existing team's technical competency along with their experience in a similar domain. Agile requires faster and continuous turnaround, which means that the development team must be competent enough to meet this requirement.

Domain Knowledge

The development team's domain knowledge is an essential requirement for the successful implementation of a project.

2. Customer Involvement

Agile Manifesto places greater emphasis on customer involvement than customer negotiation. They are some sub-factors that decide the resources, scope, and clarifications necessary for expediting the project.

Collaboration

Agile Manifesto focuses on earning customer satisfaction through early and continuous delivery. This requires customers' active participation in the project, physical availability, and high motivation towards project goals.

Commitment

Customer commitment can play a crucial role when choosing an Agile methodology. When customers aren't committed, it has a negative impact on methodologies, such as XP.

Domain knowledge is important because without clarifying the functionalities from the customer end, your project implementation can be affected.

3. Organizational Culture

Choosing an Agile project methodology depends on the prevalent culture in an organization. The pace at which a company adapts to an Agile methodology depends on how flexible it is. Typically, organizational culture can be random, hierarchical, synchronous, and collaborative. Additionally, the culture dimensions play a crucial role in choosing the Agile method. These dimensions include hierarchical, democratic, clan, and disciplined. In most cases, democratic culture is ideal for Agile project methodologies.

4. Project Nature

Agile software development can be complicated as team sizes can differ, and projects may have varying levels of criticalities. There are three sub-factors that you need to consider.

Size

The Agile project methodology is often considered ideal for medium-sized projects, owing to its testing phases. Therefore, testing carries weight as performing fast and continuous smoke and unit testing in a small project can be managed easily when compared to a larger project.

When a project is large, it needs different testing, such as integration and hardware testing. Testing Agile methodologies are not always well-fitted or feasible. For instance, FDD is ideal for teams with more than 40 members, whereas Scrum is better for teams having less than ten members.

Criticality

Project criticality is an essential metric that compares the project's cost. Therefore, if the suitable Agile methodology is not chosen as per criticality, it can dramatically raise the cost of the project. For instance, critical projects often use FDD.

Project Constraints

Scope, cost, value, and delivery date are essential considerations for project implementation. When a methodology is picked while keeping these factors in mind, it determines how successfully a project is implemented.

| CONCLUSION

Agile project management was needed due to the rising failures of the waterfall as well to benefit from the iterative approaches. It can be traced back to the 1950s, became mature in the 1990s, and was adopted in the 2000s.

The business environment is more dynamic than it ever was. Changes occur every minute, and in development, they come up every second. As one thing is completed, another task is added to the project. The agile project management is detailed, underlines all the activities, and runs the complete project. Software development is complex, but with Agile, teams receive much-needed support that empowers them to complete the projects in time.

You can still follow the waterfall methodology, but the Agile project management methodology should be preferred if you are looking to improve business performance. It allows you to work in iterations, offers constant client feedback, and reduces hassle for the project members. Software products are divided into sprints, ably supported by different stakeholders who handle the complete process.

There are some organizations that are still struggling to adapt to Agile processes. This happens when some of them adopt superficial agility without proper understanding or communication. Prioritizing practice over outcome is one of the major reasons why Agile adoption struggles. Keep in mind that Agile is simply a solution that can achieve an outcome; it depends on the organization to identify what needs to be achieved and how to implement Agile for meeting that outcome.

Agile project management has a crucial role to play in the future. Although the Agile manifesto concentrates on software development, the real Agile concept is far-reaching. It's a philosophy that focuses on empowered people and their interactions. It adds value to enterprises through early and continuous delivery. The best Agile practices are extremely disciplined and should be incorporated into corporate procedures like governance. Agile continues to surge in popularity among enterprises and even the public sector, finance, and other conservative businesses are adopting it.

The fact that Agile is steadily expanding and penetrating different areas of an organization, not just IT-related projects, should not come as a surprise. For example, small, cross-functional teams are good at generating benefits early and repeatedly. You can apply this concept throughout the company, including the end-users in the design and implementation of products and services, whereas small teams help with reducing red tape. Whenever customers are kept in the loop, quality is guaranteed.

Hence, Agile has much to offer to the wider enterprise and it's possible a time comes when Agile principles are used for running the whole organization.

- Acceptance Criteria – Set of conditions that a software product needs to meet so it is accepted by a system, customer, or user.
- Automated Testing – A form of testing where software tools are used to automate test cases.
- Beta System – A software phase where the system is still undergoing testing.
- Bug – A flaw or error in a computer program.
- Bug Report – A document containing stack traces, device logs, and diagnostic information.
- Business Requirements – Requests provided by the end-user to meet organizational goals.
- CASE – Tools used for automating assistance in software development.
- Configuration Management – Tracking and controlling changes in the project.
- Cross-Functional Team – A group of people with different expertise who are working closely to achieve common goals.
- Database Refactoring – A change in database schema intended for enhancing its design without compromising informational and behavioral semantics.
- Design Document – A document written by software developers to provide guidance to software architecture.
- Enterprise System – A large and complex software application.

- Flowchart – A graphical representation of a complex process that shows all the actions in a sequence.
- High-Level Design – Represents the system's view at an abstract level, showing how major components fit together and interact with each other.
- IDE – Stands for integrated development environment. It allows developers to write computer programs by offering a wide range of features and tools.
- Integration Testing – A form of testing where multiple software modules are tested together.
- Iterative Approach – A software approach that breaks down a large application into smaller chunks.
- Just in Time – A production model where items are generated to meet demand.
- Machine Learning – A branch of artificial intelligence that enables systems to automatically learn from history without explicit instructions.
- Object Model – Defines a project in terms of objects and classes.
- Project Lifecycle – Description of a project from start to finish.
- Project Postmortem – A process performed at the end of a project to constructively evaluate a software.
- Project Scope – It involves assessing and documenting project goals, tasks, cost, deadlines, and deliverables.
- Prototype Testing – Used to test a software in detail before its release.

- Rational Unified Process – A customizable and iterative model used to implement proven software approaches.
- Recommendation System – A software that predicts customer preferences based on their history.
- Review Meeting – A meeting organized to discuss the software's development and performance.
- Scalability – The ability of a system to manage workloads in size or scale.
- Smoke Testing – A form of testing used to determine whether the project is stable or not.
- Software Development Life Cycle (SDLC) – A systematic process for building high-quality software.
- Spaghetti Diagram - A Lean tool used for tracking products and people.
- Spiral Model – A software approach that combines the waterfall and iterative model.
- System Testing - A form of testing where a system's compliance with specific requirements is tested.
- Technical Review – A white-box testing approach used to identify defects early in the project lifecycle.
- Technical Specification – Refers to a software's customer technical requirements.
- Test-Driven Development – A form of development where testing is incorporated throughout the design and coding phases in the form of unit tests.
- Test Plan – A document used in software testing that describes the objectives, processes, and resources of a software.
- Unit Testing – A form of testing where individual software modules are tested.

- Waterfall Methodology – An old approach to software development that follows a linear sequential flow.
- Workflow Diagram – Depicts multiple actions that specify how work is done in a project.